Contents

Written by
Jillian Powell

Illustrated by
Jay Birks

Series editor **Dee Reid**

Before reading

My Super Secret School Diary

Characters

Me (Bradley)

Abby

Tricky words

ch1	p3	secondary	ch2	p10	kneeling
ch1	p5	embarrassing	ch3	p14	weird
ch1	p6	worrying	ch4	p18	wheelbarrow
ch2	p9	cupboard			

Story starter

My name is Bradley Hobbs and this is my secret diary. My best friend, Abby and I went for a look round the secondary school where we are going next term. A boy called Dillon showed us round. All the pupils looked so cool. Abby says she has a plan to make me more cool.

My
Super Secret
School Diary

Chapter One

Wednesday 4th July

Abby and I went to look round our new secondary school today. A boy called Dillon showed us round. He showed us the sports centre and the computer room. The whole school looks amazing. Even the toilets look amazing.

The only problem is the pupils. They all look so COOL. Their hair is cool. They wear their shirt collars turned up so their uniform looks cool. They do cool sports like basketball and judo. They all have the latest cool phones.

It's a nightmare, because I am not cool.

I told Gran about it when I got home.
She keeps calling it Big School. I wish
she wouldn't. It's embarrassing. I called
Abby. She kept saying how cool everyone
looked. Abby gives everyone a 'Cool
Score', to show how cool they are. She
said everyone at the new school would
get a Cool Score of ten out of ten.

That just made me feel worse. I asked Abby what my Cool Score would be. I thought she would say at least three or four. She thought about it then said, "About two." That made me feel EVEN worse!

Abby said I should stop worrying. I just need to make my Cool Score better. Then she said she has a plan. She is going to help me become cool.

Chapter Two

Thursday 5th July

This is Abby's plan:

1. Abby will let Tiddler, our class hamster, out of his cage tomorrow.
2. Everyone will be upset. They will think Tiddler is lost, or stolen, or dead.
3. I will catch Tiddler and take him back to his cage.
4. Everyone will think I'm a superhero. My Cool Score will go up to ten.

Friday 6th July

We tried out Abby's plan. This is what happened:

Abby let Tiddler out IN THE GIRLS' TOILETS! A girl from Year 3 came out screaming that she had seen a rat. I went in to catch Tiddler. Then Miss Taylor came in and found me creeping around on the floor.

"Bradley Hobbs," she yelled. "Get out of here at once!"

Miss Taylor only calls me by my full name when she is really cross. She said I had to miss playtime.

Later on, Abby passed me a note. It said, "Tiddler is in the games cupboard."

Tiddler is in the games cupboard. Abby

So I went to the games cupboard at lunchtime. Tiddler had chewed through the bean bags, and all the beans had spilled on the floor. There was no sign of Tiddler.

Then Miss Taylor came in and found me kneeling in the mountain of beans. She was REALLY cross and said I had to miss the rest of lunch break. At the end of lunch I went back to the games cupboard and found Tiddler sleeping there. I took him back to his cage.

Everyone clapped when they saw Tiddler but I must have had beans from the bean bags in my hair because Lucy Morris suddenly shouted out, "Bradley Hobbs has got giant nits!" Now my Cool Score is about one.

Chapter Three

Saturday 7th July

I watched a football match
on TV this afternoon.
The goalkeeper had
really cool hair. It was
spiky and black and
shiny. I wish I could
make my hair look
like his.

I phoned Abby to ask her what
colour she would say my hair was.
She said, "Mousey."
Who wants hair the colour of a mouse?
Then Abby said, "Why don't you dye
your hair?"
I thought it would be really cool to have
hair the same colour as the goalie.
Abby's gran is a hairdresser. She has her
own salon. So Abby and I have a new
plan. When our grans go out to lunch
together tomorrow, Abby will dye my hair.

We sneaked into Abby's gran's salon. It is amazing. It has great big mirrors and lights and chairs that you can spin round. Abby said, "Show me the colour you want your hair." I showed her a photo of the goalie and she mixed up some weird stuff. She rubbed it into my hair and put some tin foil on my head. Then she pushed a heat lamp behind me.

"How do you know how long to leave the dye on?" I asked.

"That's easy," she said. "Gran has a timer that goes ping."

It was boring just waiting, so Abby read a magazine and I played on my games console. I want to get to level 6 in Dinosaur Wars. I began to feel a bit hot under the heat lamp.

I said to Abby, "Isn't it about time that thing went ping?"

Abby said, "Oh, I forgot to put the timer on! Let's have a look."

She took the foil off and said, "Oh no!"

I looked in the mirror and saw what had happened. My hair had gone purple!

Chapter Four

Monday 9th July

Abby's gran was very angry with us. She said we have to sweep up hair in the salon every Saturday for three weeks, but she did sort out my purple hair. Now it's mousey brown again. Maybe mousey colour isn't so bad after all.

Year 2 had their sports day today. Year 6 were their Team Leaders. They were going to do long jump and high jump and races round the field. Then it rained. The sports field looked like a swamp.

"What a shame," Miss Taylor said. "Year 2 won't get their sports day."

I said to Miss Taylor, "Why don't we do some indoor races?"

She said, "Good idea."

So I got some spoons and ping pong balls and got Year 2 to do egg and spoon races. Then I got some bin bags and they did sack races. I got some skipping ropes and they did three-legged races. We had hopping races, backwards races and wheelbarrow races. Year 2 loved it.

Tuesday 10th July

Something amazing happened today. In assembly, Miss Hooper, the Year 2 class teacher, stood up and said, "Year 2 want to thank Year 6 for saving our sports day. We want to say an extra special thank you to Bradley Hobbs, the best team leader ever."

They think I am the best team leader ever! Then I heard a girl from Year 2 say "Bradley Hobbs is really cool." Abby said my Cool Score had gone up to eight. Maybe I CAN be cool at my new school (even if my hair is mousey).

I tried my new blazer on today and turned my shirt collar up. It looked quite cool on me. I am starting to look forward to next term now.

Quiz

Text detective

p4 Why did Bradley think it would be a nightmare at his new school?

p7 What was Abby's plan to make Bradley cool?

p11 Why did Lucy Morris say Bradley had nits?

p17 Why did Bradley think that mousey hair colour wasn't so bad after all?

p19 How did Bradley become a hero?

Word detective

p4 What is the effect of the repetition of the adjective 'cool'?

p10 Why is the word 'really' in capital letters?

p10 What metaphor does the author use to describe how many beans have spilled out of the bean bags?

What do you think?

Is Bradley cool? What evidence is there for and against? Does it matter whether he is cool?

HA! HA!

Q: Why did the teacher marry the caretaker?

A: Because he swept her off her feet!

Meet Your Buddy

Characters

- **Dillon** – a Year 11 pupil
- **Bradley** – a Year 6 pupil
- **Abby** – Bradley's friend, also in Year 6

Setting the scene

Dillon will be Bradley and Abby's buddy in their new school. He is showing them round. Abby and Bradley ask him questions. Bradley feels worried about fitting in.

Meet Your Buddy

Dillon: I'm Dillon. I will be your buddy when you start Year 7.

Bradley: Oh! My Gran used to have a dog called Dillon!

Abby: Be quiet, Bradley!

Dillon: You go to Hill Primary, don't you?

Bradley: Yes, that's what it says on my jumper!

Abby: Bradley, don't be so rude!

Dillon: I went to Hill Primary too. It's a good school but I like this school better.

(They go to see the playground.)

Abby: Do you have to miss play if you're in trouble?

Dillon: If you're in trouble you might get detention or you might have to do school service.

Bradley: What's school service?

Dillon: Things like picking up litter in the playground.

Abby: Oh, that doesn't sound too bad. Is detention horrible?

Dillon: It's a bit boring, but it's not too bad. We get house points for good work too.

Bradley: Why would you point at houses?

Abby: Bradley! Don't be silly! Houses are kind of like teams.

Bradley: Oh. What do you get house points for?

Dillon: Lots of things. I get a lot for sports. I am the rugby team captain.

Abby: Wow, that is cool! Can we see the sports centre now?

(They start walking to the sports centre.)

Dillon: Of course. We do so many amazing sports here, like rugby and basketball and judo.

Bradley: I don't like rugby!

Dillon: We do football too. We have boys' and girls' football teams.

Abby: That's even cooler! I'd love to play football!

Bradley: Me too. I love football!

Abby: He means he loves *watching* football on TV.

Bradley: No, I like to play too. I am pretty good in goal.

Dillon: Good. We always need more football players. Now let's go to the music centre.

Abby: What sort of music do you do here?

Dillon: We do all sorts! There are clubs and we have a school band.

Bradley: I suppose you play in the band too, Dillon?

Dillon: Yes, I play the drums.

Abby: Oh, wow, that's so …

Bradley: … cool?

Dillon: Well, you have seen everything now.

Abby: Thanks, Dillon. It all looks amazing! I can't wait to start school here!

Bradley: Hmm. Thanks, Dillon.

Dillon: That's OK! I will look out for you next term.

Abby: Why aren't you more excited, Bradley? Dillon was really nice and …

Bradley: … and cool?

Abby: Yes. What's wrong with that?

Bradley: They all look so cool. How am I ever going to fit in here? I can't play drums and I don't like rugby. I don't even *look* cool like they do.

Abby: So? You could be cool too, Bradley. We just need a plan.

Quiz

Play detective

p23 How can you tell Abby is embarrassed by Bradley?

p24 Why do you think Bradley asks a silly question?

p25 Which two words are in the contraction 'I'd'?

p26 Find a word that means the same as 'enthusiastic'.

p27 Why is Bradley not so excited about starting at the new school?

Before reading

The Rule Spinner

Setting the scene

All schools have rules that everyone must obey. Sometimes it might be fun to think about playing around with them. In this poem, the poet imagines putting school rules in a spinner, mixing them all up and seeing what funny rules come out.

Poem top tip

Look for the rhyming words at the end of the lines. Can you see a pattern?

Quiz

Poem detective

▸ Who is the speaker in this poem? How do they feel about school rules?

▸ Do you think the speaker is serious about mixing up the rules? How can you tell?

▸ How would you sum up the tone of the poem?

▸ What is the rhyming pattern?

The Rule Spinner

In school we have lots of rules.
No mobile phones! Don't talk!
Don't scribble on the desks and
in corridors, *Please walk!*

I'd put rules in a spinner,
And when the rules were spun,
They would be mixed together,
And rules would be more fun!

Instead of *No mobile phones*,
I'd say *Please send lots of texts!*
Instead of *Don't scribble!*
I'd say *Scribble on the desks!*

I'd put rules in a spinner,
And when the rules were spun,
They would be mixed together,
And rules would be more fun!

When we're in the corridor
I'd say *Everyone must run!*
The best rule of all would be …
Everyone have fun!

by Jillian Powell

Before reading
Victorian Punishments

Find out about

▶ What punishments were used in Victorian schools

▶ How some schools used leg stocks and finger stocks for children who did not sit still

▶ Why you would not want to talk in class in Victorian times

Tricky words

p31	Victorian	p31	punishments
p31	naughty	p36	leather
p31	different		

Text starter

Victorian schools were very different from schools today. Teachers were very strict and punishments were hard. Teachers sometimes put naughty children's legs or fingers in stocks. This was very painful. Children who had not done their work well might be made to wear a Dunce cap and stand in the corner.

Victorian Punishments

Victorian Schools

If you are naughty in school, you may have to miss playtime. If you had gone to school in Victorian times (1837–1901), you wouldn't have got off so easily. You may have been beaten with a cane or been put in the stocks!

Victorian schools were very different from schools today. In Victorian schools teachers were very strict and punishments were hard.

The Stocks

Leg stocks

Children who had been naughty in class were put in the stocks. They had to sit with their legs in wooden stocks until the teacher let them out. If there were no stocks in the classroom, children had to kneel on the wooden floor with their hands on the back of their neck.

Finger stocks

Children who did not keep still in Victorian times had to sit with their hands on their head for hours.

Sometimes teachers put children's fingers in finger stocks and strapped their arms behind their backs. Finger stocks were wooden blocks with holes. You couldn't move your fingers in the blocks. Your fingers hurt. You had to stand and face the wall of the classroom.

Finger stocks

Caps and Cages

The Dunce Cap

The Dunce cap was a tall cap with the letter D for Dunce on it. A Dunce was someone who was lazy or someone who had not done good work. A Dunce had to sit or stand on the Dunce's stool in a corner or face the wall of the classroom and wear the Dunce cap.

The Cage

The cage was a big basket that could be pulled up above the classroom on ropes. Naughty children had to get into the cage and stay in it until the teacher let them go.

The Punishment Book

Teachers kept a punishment book. This was a book of children's names and all the punishments they had been given. Children had to show their report from the punishment book when they left school to find a job.

Painful Punishments

The Cane

Teachers punished children by hitting them with a cane on their bottoms, hands or the back of their legs. Some teachers used a rod made from a bundle of twigs that they kept in a jar of water to keep them bendy. Other teachers used leather straps, wooden paddles or rulers.

Back boards

Are you sitting up straight? Children who did not sit up straight at their desks were given a wooden back board. They had to keep it under their arms or have it strapped to them all day, to make them sit or stand up straight.

The Log

Children who had been talking in class were sometimes made to carry a log on their back. They had to keep it on all day or until the teacher took it off.

Then and Now

In Victorian times, life was very different for children in many ways. Many children had to go out to work to help their families. Those who did go to school had hard punishments if they were naughty.

Which Victorian punishments do you think were the worst? What sort of punishments do you think work best to get children to behave and do their best in school?

In some schools and in prisons, children were hit with a rod like this one.

Quiz

Text detective

p32 Do you think after wearing finger stocks you would sit still in class in the future?

p34 How do you think children felt who had to wear the Dunce cap?

p36 Do you think it was right that teachers could use painful punishments?

p37 Why do you think teachers insisted that children sat up straight in class?

Non-fiction features

p36 Think of a caption for this photo.

p37 Why has the author used a question at the start of this page?

p38 Why is the heading suitable for the paragraph on this page?

What do you think?

Was it fair that children had to show their report from the punishment book when they left school to find a job?

HA! HA!

Q: Why did the teacher wear sunglasses?

A: Because his pupils were so bright!

Published by Pearson Education Limited, a company incorporated in England and Wales, having its registered office at Edinburgh Gate, Harlow, Essex, CM20 2JE.
Registered company number: 872828

www.pearsonschools.co.uk

Pearson is a registered trademark of Pearson plc

Text © Pearson Education Limited 2013

The right of Jillian Powell to be identified as the author of this work has been asserted by her in accordance with the Copyright, Designs and Patents Act 1988.

First published 2013

18 17 16 15 14 13
10 9 8 7 6 5 4 3 2 1

British Library Cataloguing in Publication Data is available from the British Library on request.

ISBN: 978 0 435 15249 9

Designed by Bigtop
Original illustrations © Pearson Education Limited 2013
Illustrated by Jay Birks
Printed and bound in Malaysia (CTP-VVP)
Font © Pearson Education Ltd
Teaching notes by Dee Reid

Acknowledgements
We would like to thank the following schools for their invaluable help in the development and trialling of this course:
Callicroft Primary School, Bristol; Castlehill Primary School, Fife; Elmlea Junior School, Bristol; Lancaster School, Essex; Llanidloes School, Powys; Moulton School, Newmarket; Platt C of E Primary School, Kent; Sherborne Abbey CE VC Primary School, Dorset; Upton Junior School, Poole; Whitmore Park School, Coventry.

The author and publisher would like to thank the following individuals and organisations for permission to reproduce photographs:

(Key: b-bottom; c-centre; l-left; r-right; t-top)

Alamy Images: travelibUK 38; **Birmingham Museums Picture Library:** Birmingham Museums Picture Library 33; **Corbis:** Corbis 36; **Getty Images:** Getty / Alexander Hohenlohe Burr 31; **Mary Evans Picture Library:** Mary Evans Picture Library 34; **Veer/Corbis:** Spectral-Design 3, 4-5, 6-7, 8-9, 10-11, 12-13, 14-15, 16-17, 18-19, 20

Cover image (diary): Veer/Corbis: happydancing

All other images © Pearson Education

Every effort has been made to trace the copyright holders and we apologise in advance for any unintentional omissions. We would be pleased to insert the appropriate acknowledgement in any subsequent edition of this publication.